Manchester

Home or away, the essential insider's
guide to city centre Manchester

wheretogomanchester.co.uk

Editor
Susie Stubbs,
creativetourist.com
Sub-editor
Helen Nugent
Contributors
Kate Feld,
Ben East,
Sian Cummins,
Chris Horkan,
Helen Nugent,
Kevin Bourke
Research
Jennifer Dean,
Thom Hetherington,
Charlotte Hitchen,
Hannah Tomlinson
Design & Illustration
Modern Designers
Photography
Tom Cockram
Jan Chlebik
Additional photography
Sebastian Matthes (p19)
Alexandra Wolkowicz (p28)
Bernt Rostad (32)
Ric Harris (p80)
Magnus Blikeng (p80)
John Lynch (86)

Printed in the UK by DXG

**Published on behalf of Manchester city centre
retailers by the Heart of Manchester Business
Improvement District (BID), with the support
of Visit Manchester.**

First edition: July 2013
ISBN 978-0-9576468-0-3

© *Heart of Manchester BID Company Ltd. 2013;*
Design & Photography © Modern Designers 2013;
Text © Creative Tourist Ltd.

Contents

Introduction

Looking for things to do in Manchester
but not sure where to go? Start here.

Look, we're all friends here. It's safe to assume that you know a thing or two about Manchester – why else would you pick up this book? You could be born and bred, or just here for the weekend. Maybe you're a student; perhaps you're here on business.

Whatever the reason, we figure you know the basics, and so we can skip over an industrial history that once made this Northern town the manufacturing darling of the world. We can pass by the mills that in turn gave rise to the sorts of politics – socialism, free trade, votes for all – that changed everything. We won't mention the "firsts", the test tubes and computers, and we'll gloss over a musical pedigree that stretches from the Hallé Orchestra to the Warehouse Project, via the Free Trade Hall and Factory. We won't even wax lyrical about the post-industrial Manchester, a city that has comprehensively crushed the "grim up north" stereotype under the heel of its new-build boot. We will instead start this book with a view – our favourite view, in fact - of the city that we call home.

To see it, you need to be up high. There's a point heading into the city from the west, between Deansgate and St. Peter's Square, where the rail and tram tracks that thread through Manchester like a steel spine lift you high up above the urban sprawl.

Image Left: North Tea Power, Tib Street

Below, the River Irwell winds out towards The Quays, a ribbon of water making its way between mills-turned-apartments, that draws close two cities that share the same boundary but different histories. River switches to canal, and now below are the staff at Dukes 92, setting out tables in Castlefield's morning sun. That same sun slants off the swaggering height of the Beetham Tower; inside, its guests look across Liverpool Road, their matutinal eyes alighting on the industrial shapes of MOSI, the Museum of Science & Industry. The tram pushes past the half-moon sweep of Manchester Central, the roads below clog with cars and, close by, trains take commuters on to Oxford Road.

It is like a child's drawing of the city. Everything's there: old architecture and ambitious high-rises, galleries and libraries, trains and rivers, the rhythmic rise and fall of railway arches. Everywhere there are people – working, moving, talking, doing.

And just as easily as a child can draw the city, so Manchester is the kind of place that is exactly what you make of it.

That's the point of this book. Not to tell you everything there is to know about Manchester, but to tell you enough to surprise you, or to remind you that there is more to see, do and enjoy in the city centre than perhaps you first thought. This book tells you about some of the places we know, and that we think you might like. The places to go, in fact, that will make this city of ours a favourite city of yours.

So – where to go? If you're not sure, this is as good a place to start as any. Like we said, we're all friends here.

1

Five not to miss
1. **Selfridges** (p47)
2. **Takk** (p59)
3. **Corridor** (p73)
4. **The Deaf Institute** (p81)
5. **The Royal Exchange** (p91)

2

1. Chancery Place (p34)
2. The Alchemist (p73)
3. The Royal Exchange (p91)

3

Districts

SALFORD

CITY CENTRE

SPINNINGFIELDS

CASTLEFIELD

DEANSGATE

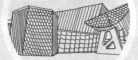

THE QUAYS

**WHITWORTH
ST WEST**

Like any city, Manchester has more quarters than is
mathematically possible. But its districts are less the product
of a developer's fevered imagination and more the result of
the organic growth of a place that is continually reinventing
itself. For this guide, we have split the city into twelve districts.

NORTHERN QUARTER

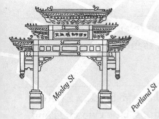

Swan St

Great Ancoats St

Newton St

PICCADILLY

Mosley St

Portland St

CHINATOWN

GAY VILLAGE

London Rd

Princess St

Fairfield St

Whitworth St

OXFORD RD

Key to this guide

CC (for City Centre)
SF (for Spinningfields)
CF (for Castlefield)
DG (for Deansgate)
WS (for Whitworth Street West)
OR (for Oxford Road)
CT (for Chinatown)
GV (for Gay Village)
PD (for Piccadilly)
NQ (for Northern Quarter)
SA (for Salford)
QU (for The Quays)

Districts

CC   *The City Centre* is the beating retail heart of Manchester that nevertheless includes such heritage highs as the Town Hall.

SF   *Spinningfields* is the new kid on the block, a £1.5bn development of high-end shops, blue chip HQs and fabulous eateries.

CF   *Castlefield* goes way back, to the Roman fort of Mamucium, via the cobbles and canals that now make it a summertime draw.

DG   *Deansgate* combines industrial heritage with entertainment, via Manchester Central, Deansgate Locks and the Bridgewater Hall.

WS   *Whitworth Street West* is home to new arts and film space HOME from 2015, and a clutch of independent bars and eateries that lead to Oxford Road Station.

OR   *Oxford Road* is all about the academia, with two universities, the Whitworth and Manchester Museum all lining its route.

CT	*Chinatown* may be less than half a mile across, but is the largest such community outside London; don't miss its New Year celebrations.
GV	*The Gay Village* is bisected by Canal Street, which gives focus to the area's many and varied bars, clubs, restaurants and places to stay.
PD	*Piccadilly* is dominated by its namesake station but also includes excellent hotels, plus Piccadilly Gardens, bars, eateries and shops.
NQ	*The Northern Quarter* is the city's creative district, its narrow lanes studded with indie boutiques, street art and hipster hang-outs.
SA	*Salford* is another city away, its traditional pubs and arts organisations coalescing around the creatively-minded Chapel Street.
QU	*The Quays* is the city's waterfront, home to MediaCityUK, The Lowry and IWM North.

One day

If you only have time to dip your toe into
Manchester, dip it in style.

Enjoy a day of the most luxurious sightseeing, supping and shopping in the city, starting with breakfast at *San Carlo Cicchetti* (p57) a suitably high-shine eatery tucked into the ground floor of *House of Fraser* (p45); despite its Italian heritage, it supplies one of the best full English efforts in the city.

Head up King Street to indulge in a little retail therapy (*Hermès, Barbour, Crombie* and *DKNY* are all on hand), before your first cultural pit stop of the day, the neo-Gothic *Manchester Town Hall*. This Grade I-listed beauty was designed by Alfred Waterhouse and is civic opulence defined (if you have room after breakfast, the *Sculpture Hall Café* (p59) serves up tea and cake among the marble statuary of Manchester's great and good).

Indulge in admiration of another kind on the way back to King Street, where *Vivienne Westwood's* boutique (p41) is housed inside another impressive building: inside, it's all baroque wood panelling and double-height ceilings. Pick up on any designer shops you missed earlier before ducking through the passageway that leads onto the graceful St. Ann's Square; here you'll find the Grade I-listed church that lends the square its name. Close by, *St. Ann's Arcade* contains street and footwear outfitters, *Ran* (p41), or try *The Avenue,* five minutes' walk along Deansgate. Here, the smart glass and steel environs of Spinningfields host flagship shops from the highest end of retail: *Mulberry* (p47) and *Emporio Armani* (p47) to name but two.

Image Left: Mulberry, The Avenue

More cerebral sights await at *The John Rylands Library* (p89), reckoned by some to be one of the world's greatest libraries. A neo-Gothic memorial to an Industrial Revolution cotton magnate, it was modelled on a traditional Oxford college library but put together on a grand Mancunian scale. Just to stand in its Reading Room, surrounded on all sides by books and statuary, is one of the greatest thrills of literary Manchester.

Turn now towards the retail delights of Exchange Square and New Cathedral Street, where *Selfridges* (p47), *Harvey Nichols* (p47) and the *Corn Exchange* (p45) all lie. Close by is what remains of medieval Manchester; both the glorious *Manchester Cathedral* and *Chetham's Library* (p89) date back to the 15th century, the latter being the oldest library in the English-speaking world. Among its readers was Karl Marx, who sat at its tables to pen the Communist Manifesto. Consider the weight of political history at *Hanging Ditch Wine Merchants* (p49), a narrow shop stacked high with the sorts of fine wines you never knew existed; enjoy a glass or two inside. Local folklore has it that Hanging Ditch was the place where local miscreants once swung for their crimes. The reality is far more prosaic: it was a ditch where textile manufacturers hung their cloths to dry.

Exhausted, or just pleasantly sozzled, head back to King Street. Opposite *Agent Provocateur* (the former Manchester Reform Club, opened by then-Prime Minister, William Gladstone in 1871, p41), you'll find *Jamie's Italian* (p65). This magnificent building was the Midland Bank; if anything has the knock 'em dead charisma to match Jamie Oliver's patented charm, this building is it. Chandeliers twinkle in its stratosphere, while its vault, lined with polished steel safety deposit boxes, whispers of the rich history that underpins this city. And surely there's no better end to a day of luxury than to dine in the home of old money?

One Night

Evening in Manchester is something else
— if you know where to go.

We suggest you begin your night by orientating yourself from above. *Cloud 23* (p73) is Manchester's most vertiginous bar, and a recent refurb has reaffirmed it as the best place to get a handle on the city below. And although it operates a guest list after 6pm, Cloud 23 is never pretentious: a pre-dinner cocktail (names such as Dalton's Atomic Experiment confirm its humour) can be the perfect livener.

Back down to earth, a short walk alongside railway arches brings you to *Gorilla* (p75) - a bar that doubles up as a kitchen, live venue and club space. Its mezzanine gin parlour is a particularly nice touch, and it's tempting to settle in for the evening: recent visitors include bands such as Frightened Rabbit, Dutch Uncles and Villagers. Gorilla's music hall sister, incidentally, is one of the best places to see live music in the city; *The Deaf Institute* (p81) is a 15-minute walk away along Oxford Road.

But much closer - a mere 50 yards away - is one of Manchester's enduring cultural hubs. *Cornerhouse* (p91) is an art-house cinema, cafe, bar and art venue rolled into one, and if your itinerary doesn't allow for time to catch the latest foreign film, then pop into its galleries, open until 8pm most days.

Image Left: The Deaf Institute, Oxford Road

By now, thoughts will inevitably turn to dinner, so swing into the city centre. If Mancunian authenticity is key, the home-made Corned Beef Hash (ten days in the making, no less) in the Dickensian surrounds of *Mr Thomas' Chop House* (p57) makes for a memorable meal. But sometimes escapism means going further than England, in which case push the boat out for *Australasia* (p65), the Spinningfields eatery that delivers a smart fusion of Pacific Rim flavour.

And if a taste of down under in the middle of Manchester sounds odd, it's not half as weird as a 16th-century oast house brought, brick by brick, from Kent and installed in a concrete courtyard. Somehow, *The Oast House* (p61) works, with its great range of ales and barbecue-based menu. Just around the corner, to complete the strangeness, is a "tiki dive bar" called *The Liars Club* (p75), current holder of Manchester Food & Drink Festival's bar of the year award and another compelling cocktail pit stop.

No late night Mancunian excursion is complete without a visit to the Northern Quarter. There are almost too many bars to list here, but modern real ale fans will love the simplicity of the Marble Brewery's *57 Thomas Street* operation; anywhere that sells a beer called Pint gets our vote, and they offer artisan cheeses to match. Nearby, *Port Street Beer House* (p71) is currently pub of the year, while, helping to soak up all that heavy ale, *Bakerie* (p61) is a "bread and wine" bar that bakes its own and is frequented with almost religious fervour by its fans. But there comes a time when sitting and sipping loses its appeal. *Black Dog Ballroom* (p75) bridges the gap between late and later, a speakeasy, diner and pool room with an excellent music policy that's open until 4am. *Common's* (p73) eclectic nights make this a regular, if intimate, haunt of Manchester's hipsters. On the opposite end of the scale, for big experiences on packed dancefloors, check *The Warehouse Project's* (p81) listings - it doesn't run throughout the year, but is all the better for it. And if you manage all that in a night, well done – and welcome to Manchester.

Five not to miss
1. Gorilla (p75)
2. The Oast House (p61)
3. Mr. Thomas' Chop House (p57)
4. Port Street Beer House (p71)
5. The Warehouse Project (p81)

1. Gorilla (p75)
2. New Cathedral St
3. The Warehouse Project (p81)

2

3

Weekend

Where old meets new:
a little over 48 hours in the city.

Friday

You've finished work and now you're standing in the city, ears
processing the rush hour thrum, brain trying to gauge where's
good to go. Head for the *Britons Protection* (p71), part pub, part
institution, which boasts some 300 varieties of whisky. You may
spot a musician or two supping a pint, here on a break from
classical music duties at the *Bridgewater Hall* (p79) opposite. Aim
for a gig there or head to the *Deaf Institute* (p81), a dancehall and
diner that's good for easy eats and raucous club nights – all within
Grade I-listed surrounds. If sleeping with historic giants is your
thing, try the *Radisson Blu Edwardian* (p95), once the Free Trade
Hall. On the same stretch of road you'll also find the grand dame
of Mancunian hospitality, the *Midland Hotel* (p95). Built in 1903 to
the tune of £1m, this lavish, Edwardian Baroque hotel is where
Rolls met Royce and a motor empire was born.

Saturday

Breakfast by the canal at *Dukes 92* (p61) before ambling around
Castlefield – and wonder at the fact that this now peaceful urban
park was once an industrial hub, the place where the Bridgewater
and Rochdale canals converged and goods were clanked and
carted into and out of the city. Keep your eyes peeled for the
weekend artisan market held here. Nearby is *MOSI*, the Museum
of Science & Industry (p89). Home to the world's first passenger
railway, it also showcases all manner of trains, planes and hands-
on science exhibits.

Image Left: The Oast House, The Avenue

1

of Daniel Libeskind's museum is based on a globe shattered by war; the architecture forms a subtly disorienting backdrop to thought-provoking displays. There's more culture at *The Lowry* (p87), the arts centre that stages outstanding theatre, comedy exhibitions and performance. Finish with modern British dining at refined restaurant close by the BBC, *Damson.*

Head now towards Deansgate Station, from where you can take the Metrolink out to The Quays, the former industrial docks which served the monumental Manchester Ship Canal. Home to *MediaCityUK* and its star tenants, BBC North and ITV Granada, there are almost daily tours of the Beeb's HQ. For eating on the hoof, try *Booths* (p63), the family-owned supermarket that gives Waitrose a run for its money. Two footbridges connect *IWM North* (p89) to the media action. The design

Sunday

Assuming you can resist the clarion call of Manchester's shopping, we suggest you head south, to *The Whitworth* (p87), a gallery in a park where the café is run by seasonal food champion, Peter Booth. The gallery closes in September 2013 for a nine month-long, £15m extension; catch it now. Happily brunched out, head down Oxford Road, stopping off for a pint at *Kro*, a Danish-inspired pub housed in the former Temperance Society building. Oh, the irony. Close by is *The Church* of the Holy Name of Jesus, featuring a cloistered interior lauded by über architectural critic, Sir Nikolaus Pevsner. It is matched in grandeur by Alfred Waterhouse's university precinct and neo-Gothic *Manchester Museum* (p89) nearby; don't miss its Living Worlds gallery, the sleek reinvention of a natural history gallery by art and fashion producers, Villa Eugénie.

Head into town, past the 175-year-old *Manchester School of Art* (graduates include L.S. Lowry), on past *Cornerhouse* (p87) and the West End delights of the *Palace Theatre* (p91), perhaps stopping off at the listed St. James' Building for an Italian gelato at *Fresco Freddo's* (p63). You're not done yet. Sitting at the end of Oxford Street like a neo-Classical full stop is *Central Library* (p89); a £48m restoration is approaching completion. Admire its restrained beauty before indulging in homemade cake (and some art, too) at neighbouring *Manchester Art Gallery* (p87). You may have noticed that we end a few minutes' walk from your hotel, so you've not far to go to collect your bags, pass go and toddle off home. We're good like that.

1. The Quays
2. The Whitworth's Café (p87)
3. Great John Street Hotel (p95)

2

3

IWM **NORTH**
IMPERIAL   WAR   MUSEUMS

IWM NORTH

DISCOVER HOW WAR SHAPES LIVES

The multi-award winning IWM North (part of Imperial War Museums), is a great FREE day out for all ages. Designed by world-renowned architect Daniel Libeskind to represent a globe shattered by conflict, it reveals how war and conflict have shaped people's lives from 1900 to now.

Take the Metrolink to MediaCityUK or Harbour City or the X50 bus

Open daily 10am – 5pm FREE ENTRY (Closed 24, 25, 26 December)

0161 836 4000
iwm.org.uk

NATIONAL FOOTBALL MUSEUM

The nation's passion plays here in Manchester.

MUCH MORE

THAN

90

MINUTES

OF

FOOTBALL

FREE ADMISSION OPEN DAILY

Open 7 days a week
Fresh food served in the cafe from 9am

Urbis Building,
Cathedral Gardens,
Manchester
M4 3BG

Follow us: @footballmuseum
facebook.com/NationalFootballMuseum
www.nationalfootballmuseum.com

Highlights

The curious and the outdoor, the high-rise
and familial: the lesser-known city.

❦

Curious

Every city has its quirks, and Manchester is no exception. Take the *Caxton's Buildings* on Piccadilly (nos. 77-83) – a fairly ordinary 19th-century building until you get to its eaves. There, perched on a ledge, sit two sandstone men, curiously kitted out in lederhosen and Alpine hats – and no one knows why. Similar mystery surrounded the appearance of mosaic *Space Invaders* across the city in 2004. They still adorn walls in the Northern Quarter (try Back Thomas Street) and behind the *Palace Theatre* (p91). Yet aside from an anonymous website, the identity of their creator remains unknown.

Manchester invented many things (computers, atomic theory, the Manchester Egg*) but it also has a stake in the humble weekend. *St. John's Gardens* (p30) displays a little-known memorial to William Marsden, who lobbied for mill workers to get a Saturday half-day holiday. Eventually adopted nationally, the weekend surely began here. The *Godlee Observatory* (Sackville Street) is similarly well hidden. Gifted to the city in 1903, it's cared for by the Manchester Astronomical Society, one of the UK's oldest. But even they aren't as venerable as the *Salford Friendly Anglers Society*. Formed in 1817, this is the world's oldest angling club; it used to meet at *The King's Arms* (p71) and catch salmon in the River Irwell.

Image Left: Chinese Arch, Chinatown

Old school too is *MOSI* (p89), home to a stretch of the world's first passenger railway line. Take a ride on this historic track – on a steam train, naturally. *Oxford Road Station*, meanwhile, is rated by Pesvner as "one of the most remarkable in the country" thanks to its ship-like, wooden structure.

Or head to Chapel Street's *Sacred Trinity* which, along with *St. Philip with St. Stephen*, is more than just a beautiful church. Both regularly host live music gigs from up-and-coming acts. St. Philip's also has a doppelgänger - its architect, Robert Smirke, built an identical church in London. Prefer the new? Though the *Beetham Tower* now only quietly resonates, for several years it "played" a musical B in high winds. *IWM North* (p89), meanwhile, is Manchester's most disorientating building: its sloping walls and floors mean there's barely a right angle in sight.

1

2

* A pickled egg wrapped in Bury black pudding and sausage meat, rolled in a golden crumb; try one at *The Mark Addy* (p57).

1. *St. Philip with St. Stephen (p81)*
2. *Caxton's Buildings*
3. *MOSI (p89)*

3

Five favourite curious

1. Godlee Observatory, 2. The Manchester Egg
(at The Mark Addy p57), 3. Corporation Street
postbox, 4. Oxford Road Station, 5. The world's
oldest angling club

Close by at The Quays, the *Detroit Bridge* may
look permanent, but was once classed as a boat.
When developers wanted to float it down the canal
to its current location near The Lowry, it had to first
apply for a maritime licence. Back in town, the 100
year-old *pillar box* on Corporation Street is made of
sterner stuff: despite being feet from the 1996 IRA
bomb that destroyed all else around, it remained
intact. This postbox was not for moving.

1

Outdoor

We'll come right out and say it: Manchester isn't renowned for its greenery. But while it may lack a central park big enough for a football match it does have plenty of pocket parks and open spaces – and it also boasts an "urban heritage park" in the form of *Castlefield*. Our favourite place to spend a sunny afternoon, the home of an outdoor arena, restaurants and weekly artisan market, this is where the bustle of the city is replaced by sleepy canal boats and the occasional tram rattling overhead.

Not far away is the quiet *St. John's Gardens* (Lower Bryom Street); a memorial notes the 22,000 people buried in this former churchyard. *Grosvenor Square* (Oxford Road) is similarly consecrated ground: it sits on the site of the former All Saints church that gives MMU's adjacent campus its name. And *St. Michael's & Angel Meadows* (off Dantzic Street) may now be a Green Flag-holding park but was once a notorious slum and the final resting place of 40,000 paupers. It's close to new Co-operative headquarters, *NOMA*, and *The Marble Arch* (p71).

The Quays is an example of how to reinvent old industrial space, the former Salford Docks reimagined as a "destination" waterfront. The wide open space of Manchester Ship Canal acts as a foil to the built-up environment that surrounds it. *Piccadilly Basin* and *Ancoats* continue the waterside theme, Piccadilly Basin's annual canal festival and waterside planting hinting at what is to come in Ancoats: here, *New Islington Marina* (Old Mill Street) and canal-side parks provide respite from the city centre that is only minutes away.

Five public spaces
1. Grosvenor Square
(Oxford Road)
2. The Quays
3. Castlefield
4. Exchange Square
5. Trinity Bridge
(St. Mary's Parsonage)

1. Cathedral Gardens (p33)
2. Castlefield

2

1

Urban is the only word to describe the Northern Quarter's *Stevenson Square*. Soon to be greened, this square is notable for the street art "exhibitions" sponsored by resident art store, *Fred Aldous* (p49). Not far away, *Exchange Square* offers a glossier interpretation of public space, its meandering water feature a contrast to the electric, retail hum of *Selfridges* (p47)

Five high-rises
1. Manchester Town Hall
2. Civil Justice Centre
3. CIS Tower
4. IWM North (p89)
5. Daily Express Building

1. Fred Aldous (p49)
2. Northern Quarter
3. Alan Turing Memorial

2

3

and the *Corn Exchange* (p45). Neighbouring *Cathedral Gardens* is a pull for families thanks to its fountain, hillocks and playground close by on Victoria Street.

There are other public squares – the busy *St. Ann's* and the civic *Albert* (the host to many a Manchester festival and fair) – and other gardens too. *Sackville Gardens* (Sackville Street) is home to a life-size bronze sculpture of computer pioneer, Alan Turing, while *Parsonage Gardens* (off Deansgate) is close to Santiago Calatrava's *Trinity Bridge*. This sinuous, pedestrian suspension bridge curves over the Irwell, connecting two cities – and leading directly to *The Lowry Hotel* (p95), from whose restaurant terrace you can most properly consider the great urban outdoors.

High-Rise

A decade or so ago, you could barely move in Manchester for building sites, the rainy city temporarily dubbed the craney city thanks to a preponderance of tower cranes. We all know what kick-started this frenetic pace of construction (whisper it: the IRA bomb), but terrorism alone can't be credited for a city whose skyline is now punctuated by ever higher new-builds – ambition and political leadership played starring roles, too. Chief among kings is Manchester's tallest, the 47-storey *Beetham Tower*.

Perhaps lesser known is Spinningfields' *Civil Justice Centre*, the first major court complex to be built in Britain in 125 years; the 17-storey centre was nicknamed the "filing cabinet" thanks to its cantilevered structure and has won a clutch of international design awards. More high-spec offices are at *Chancery Place*, a 14-storey block tucked behind King Street. Its full height curtain glazing acts as a mirror for the Gothic Victorian buildings surrounding it. Chancery Place's triangular footprint faintly echoes that of Urbis, now the *National Football Museum* (p89), while at The Quays, both *The Lowry* (p87) and *IWM North* (p89) have multiple architectural awards to their names. Try the latter's tower for a vertiginous view. *The Bridgewater Hall* (p79), meanwhile, may not shout quite as loudly but is the cleverest of the lot. Purpose-built in 1996, it floats on earthquake-proof isolation bearings so that the music played within is insulated from the noise without.

1. *IWM North (p89)*
2. *Beetham Tower*
3. *Manchester Town Hall*

34

2

3

Yet for all this recent work, high-rises here are nothing new. For years, the 1962 *CIS Tower* was the city's highest; this Co-op building is notable now for being clad in solar panels. The *Daily Express Building* on Great Ancoats Street is even older. This Art Deco block with a curved, black glass exterior, opened in 1939. Or consider a trio constructed by celebrated Victorian architect, Alfred Waterhouse: *Manchester Town Hall*, a Grade I-listed neo-Gothic monument to the city's industrial ambition, *Manchester Museum* (p89), and the stouter *41 Spring Gardens*, once the National Provincial Bank. The latter is one of a clutch of former financial institutions that left an upward architectural mark on the city – including *Jamie's Italian* (p65) opposite, once the Midland Bank, and whose soaring interior was designed by Edward Lutyens. So from new to old, high to mid-rise, it seems that Manchester has always been on the up.

Family

Lately Manchester has become a draw for families looking for something to do. Exhibit A is the city's first playground, handily located next to the main shopping district and the ever-popular *National Football Museum* (p89). We recommend picnicking in nearby *Cathedral Gardens* (and frolicking in its sweet stream and fountains), but if the rainy city is living up to its name, *Tampopo* and *Croma* pizzeria are safe bets for child-friendly dining.

If you're planning an outing with kids and babies in tow, hit Castlefield and Spinningfields. You're never far from a good place to burn off some energy – feeding ducks in the canal, exploring Roman ruins, or running about in Hardman Square – while the child-friendly *Carluccio's* is on hand for snacks and drinks. The small people in your life can also go wild at *MOSI* (p89). As well as trains, planes and automobiles, its Experiment! gallery is full

1. People's History Museum (p89)
2. BBC North (www.bbc.co.uk/tours)
3. MOSI (p89)

of interactive exhibits, or else try the hands-on activities and holiday workshops at *People's History Museum* (p89) close by. And there's a busy calendar of outdoor events here too, such as an Easter duck race and children's films at Spinningfields' seasonal outdoor cinema, *Screenfields*. Oxford Road is another reliable family destination. Your little creatures can admire dinosaur skeletons, Egyptian mummies and stuffed animals at *Manchester Museum* (p89), while, further along the same stretch of road, *The Whitworth* (p87) has won awards for an under 5's programme that turns every visit into a creative adventure. It's also home to an unusually good café serving healthy kids' meals. If it's warm out, eat your lunch in the adjacent *Whitworth Park*. Up for an adventure? Head to Manchester's waterfront, The Quays, where you can cruise the waterways on a boat tour or try climbing and kayaking at *Salford Watersports Centre*. The Quays is also home to

3

two institutions with great kids' offerings – *The Lowry* (p87) and *IWM North* (p89) – as well as the cricket and football grounds at *Old Trafford* (the latter complete with its own museum dedicated to Manchester United. Manchester City's *Etihad Stadium,* on the other side of the city, also runs regular family events and tours). And don't forget the *BBC North's* base at MediaCityUK; it's open for tours five days a week (ages 9 and up). Just the place for budding TV talent.

Shop

Boutique, for him, high street, high end
and one off shopping.

Manchester may be known for many things, but while some might visit for the beautiful game (and others for business or a legendary night out), many more pitch up here in order to get their retail kicks. It's hardly surprising. The compact nature of the city centre means that you can browse the Northern Quarter boutiques, flash your cash at The Avenue, dip into the pocket-sized arcades off St. Ann's Square, lose yourself inside Manchester Arndale or dive into the departments of Harvey Nichols – all in one day. In between the retail cracks you might stumble upon gallery shops, seasonal markets, contemporary craft outlets and the odd curiosity. Manchester has more ways of relieving you of your readies than there are sunglasses in Selfridges – but we guarantee that while you'll leave with a lighter wallet it won't be long before you're yearning to return. This is our guide to help you make the most of your visit.

For full shop listings and offers go to visitmanchester.com/shopping and follow @shopmcr

Image Left: Vivienne Westwood, Spring Gardens

1

2

3

Dedicated followers of fashion, pay attention: Manchester does a brilliant line in boutiques, the majority of which understand that looking good goes hand in hand with attentive, friendly service. Many cluster around the narrow lanes of the city's Northern Quarter but you'll find more tucked along King Street or close to St. Ann's Square – and even, in one case, masquerading as a megastore on Market Street. For clues as to stores that stock unusual, small and independent labels, read on.

– Boutique –

CURIOUSER AND CURIOUSER [1]

This pretty shop supplies understated womenswear and accessories with the emphasis on the casual. Labels are sourced from around the world, yet are surprisingly affordable.
35 Tib St, M4 1LX (NQ)
curiouserboutique.co.uk

–

VIVIENNE WESTWOOD

Our Viv's Manchester store comes complete with carved mahogany panelling and double-height ceilings, a luxe backdrop to the sharply-crafted mens and womenswear on offer.
47 Spring Gardens, M2 2BG (CC)
viviennewestwood.co.uk

–

RAN

Tucked inside a tiny arcade off St. Ann's Square, Ran is a shop of two halves: unisex footwear on one side and achingly fashionable streetwear from the likes of Obey, Comune and Fred Perry are on the other.
7 & 8 St Ann's Arcade, M2 7HQ (CC)
ranshop.co.uk

–

URBAN OUTFITTERS

This five-floor megastore manages, despite its size, to offer one of the best ranges of boutique labels in the city – such as Cheap Monday and Herschel.
41-43 Market St, M1 1WR (CC)
urbanoutfitters.co.uk

–

AGENT PROVOCATEUR [2]

As famous for its provocative window displays as it is for sumptuous lingerie, rest assured that service here is discreet – whether you're after new kecks or a diamanté-encrusted riding whip.
81 King St, M2 4AH (CC)
agentprovocateur.com

–

SPACE NK

A high-end apothecary where attentive service, skincare brands such as Eve Lom, Sai-Sei and NARS, and a bright, space-age interior make you feel that anything, or at least airbrushed perfection, is possible.
5 St Ann's Sq, M2 7LP (CC)
uk.spacenk.com

–

HERMÈS [3]

Silk and cashmere scarves, fine leather belts and bags, and a store shot through with a classic, equestrian flavour - Hermès is the go-to boutique for the highest class of accessories.
31 King St, M2 6AA (CC)
uk.hermes.com

–

CAMPER

A narrow slip of a shop, artfully filled with top-lit men's, women's and kids' shoes. Everything on sale in Camper bears the trademark style and wit of this Spanish footwear maker.
8 Exchange St, M2 7HA (CC)
camper.com

–

How often have you heard that shopping is a woman's game? Those pedalling that particular line have clearly not meandered Manchester's streets lately: retail here is split fairly evenly between shops catering solely for women and those aimed squarely at men. There's everything along the masculine fashion spectrum, from the urban classics which make the Northern Quarter a hipster haven to the stiff upper lip outfitters found on King Street and beyond. Read on for our recommendations.

OI POLLOI [3]

This indie outfitter is beloved of those after carefully crafted menswear with an urban edge. Expect parkas by Penfield and Harringtons from Baracuta, or choose from Fox umbrellas (rain) and Clarks Originals desert boots (shine).

63 Thomas St, M4 1LQ (NQ)
oipolloi.com

–

JAMES DARBY [1]

James Darby's handmade attire, using classic English wools and tweed, have a contemporary feel that sets them apart from the standard three-piece suit.

40 Thomas St, M4 1ER (NQ)
jamesdarbybespoke.com

–

CROMBIE

It may be known the world over for its British-made, three-quarter length coats, luxury menswear and accessories, but Crombie only has three standalone stores worldwide – this is one of them.

33 King St, M2 6AA (CC)
crombie.co.uk

–

WOOD

This streetwear store stocks sweats, hoodies, high tops and baseball caps from the likes of 10 Deep, Publish, Herschel and Stussy; a Northern Quarter staple.

55 Oldham St, M1 1JR (NQ)
ashopcalledwood.com

–

BARBOUR [2]

Tucked next to Hermès, this dedicated boutique majors on the quilted jackets and gilets that made Barbour's name, alongside vintage-styled motorcycle jackets, shirts and tees.

5 St Ann's Passage, M2 6AD (CC)
barbour.com

–

THOMAS PINK

The floor-to-ceiling wooden shelves offer an unrivalled choice of formal shirts. With neighbouring Charles Tyrwhitt, this is a formidable foray into the world of sharp corporate dressing.

58 King St, M2 4LY (CC)
thomaspink.com

–

BENCH

Originating from the Madchester music scene in the 1980s, Bench went on to become a global streetwear brand - this recently renovated store with basement gallery reminds you why.

59 Church St, M4 1PD (NQ)
bench.co.uk

–

HIGH & MIGHTY

Above average? This is the store for you. Clothes, shoes, accessories and even made-to-measure suits are on offer for those whose stature exceeds expectations.

55 King St, M2 4LQ (CC)
highandmighty.co.uk

–

1

2

3

The high street in Manchester focuses on Market Street, the pedestrianised shopping boulevard around which every high street brand you can imagine coalesces – with a few more thrown in to boot. With Piccadilly Gardens at one end and St Ann's Square at the other, Market Street is always heaving, its flagship stores and big name brands equalled by the vast Manchester Arndale mall that towers over the action. If you're struggling to find what you're looking for, try our suggestions on for size.

MANCHESTER ARNDALE [1]

Whatever you want, it's got to be under this one roof. Manchester Arndale is home to 240 stores, including flagship branches of Next, Domo, Topshop and Oasis, all spread across one of Europe's biggest shopping centres.

Market St, M4 3AQ (CC)
manchesterarndale.com

–

CORN EXCHANGE [2]

Recently re-branded and sitting inside a Grade II-listed building, shop here for contemporary jewellery at Green + Benz, or rifle the luxurious racks at Jigsaw.

Exchange Sq, M4 3TR (CC)
cornexchangemanchester.co.uk

–

HOUSE OF FRASER

Manchester's oldest department store boasts a dazzling array of cult brands and high street favourites over eight floors, from Mac and Mulberry to Whistles and Lulu Guinness.

98-116 Deansgate, M3 4QL (DG)
houseoffraser.co.uk

–

TOPSHOP & TOPMAN

These Northern flagship stores are shopping nirvana for fashionistas seeking everything from catwalk-inspired trends and boutique concessions to an eye-watering choice of shoes.

Manchester Arndale, M4 3AQ (CC)
topshop.com, topman.com

–

WATERSTONES

As bookshops go, Waterstones takes some beating. Manchester's biggest specialist bookshop stocks 100,000 titles spread over three floors. Or try the sister store in Manchester Arndale.

91 Deansgate, M3 2BW (DG)
waterstones.com

–

DEBENHAMS

Debenhams stands proud at the top of Market Street, a Manchester landmark that offers a wide range of Designers at Debenhams including Jasper Conran, Betty Jackson and John Rocha.

Market St, M60 1TA (PD)
debenhams.com

–

MARKS AND SPENCER

Once the largest M&S in the world, this store still packs a punch, from good quality frocks, nicks and socks to the homeware smorgasbord on the top floor. A new food hall and café add to the mix.

7 Market St, M1 1WT (CC)
marksandspencer.com

–

MANCHESTER ARNDALE MARKET [3]

This covered market is a cornucopia of reasonably-priced food and stalls selling all manner of clothes and accessories – and a myriad of other products too numerous to mention.

49 High St, M4 3AH (CC)
manchesterarndale.com

1

2

3

Looking for a retail fix closer to the top end of the scale? Get a refined shopping boost courtesy of the stores that line King Street, the historic home of high end shopping in Manchester. Or head towards New Cathedral Street where the joys of Harvey Nichols and Selfridges are supplemented by other luxurious retailers. And if you're not spent up, five minutes' walk away is newly-minted The Avenue, which supplies the threads for the sharp-suited and booted of Spinningfields.

EMPORIO ARMANI [1]

Housed in one of the swankiest buildings on top shopping street The Avenue, this flagship outlet of Emporio Armani represents high-end retail at its best.
The Avenue, M3 3AE (SF)
armani.com

–

SELFRIDGES [2]

Selfridges has just four stores in Britain – and two of them are in Manchester. Lose yourself in the newly-renovated beauty hall or dive in to a delectable range of world-famous brands.
1 Exchange Sq, M3 1BD (CC)
selfridges.com

–

MULBERRY

This sister to London's flagship store is chock-full of lovely things, among them its renowned and quintessentially English belted macs, tailored trousers and leather gloves.
The Avenue, M3 3FL (SF)
mulberry.com

–

HARVEY NICHOLS

Harvey Nichols is unalloyed shopping pleasure. This branch, spread over three levels, is a retail oasis. Be sure to check out the heavenly Jo Malone concession on the ground floor.
21 New Cathedral St, M1 1AD (CC)
harveynichols.com

–

RADLEY

The Radley signature dog prints make this store stand out. Simple, stylish and coveted by lovers of handbags everywhere, head here to pick up a new accessory.
8 New Cathedral St, M1 1AD (CC)
radley.co.uk

–

BELSTAFF [3]

Belstaff is a brand steeped in British heritage and best known for producing all-weather jackets for bikers and is currently the clothing of choice for the Hollywood set.
76-80 King St, M2 4NH (CC)
belstaff.co.uk

–

DKNY

Although there are plenty of places to indulge a love of Donna Karan's wares, this deceptively large store specialising in in carefully-constructed casualwear makes for the best shopping experience.
76-80 King St, M2 4NH (CC)
dkny.com

–

TOMMY HILFIGER

Tommy Hilfiger sits cheek by jowl with a collection of other upmarket clothes shops on King Street. College jackets, polo neck tees and chinos – all of Hilfiger's signature designs can be purchased here.
51 King St, M2 7AZ (CC)
uk.tommy.com

–

Some of Manchester's most glorious stores are off the beaten retail track – but hunting down such unusual shops is worth the effort. On top of personalised service, many of these one-off boutiques can tell a tale or two and demonstrate an independent streak that's in keeping with a city which, as a whole, doesn't like to tread a well-worn path. From bespoke beer and kitchen kit to flower emporiums and craft centres, here is our selection.

– One Off –

HANGING DITCH WINE MERCHANTS [3]

A specialist wine store stacked floor-to-ceiling with one of the largest selections of fine wines in the city, stop here for a glass or two while you choose between a Chablis or a Chardonnay.

42-44 Victoria St, M3 1ST (CC)
hangingditch.com

–

MAGMA

The graphic designer's bookstore of choice, expect unusual and rare magazine titles, style bibles and books on art, design and illustration from this independent outlet.

22 Oldham St, M1 1JN (NQ)
magmabooks.com

–

FROG

A boutique florists selling the most beautiful blooms, you can be assured of contemporary arrangements and floral works of art; or try Northern Flower on nearby Tib Street.

51 Turner St, M4 1DN (NQ)
frogflowers.co.uk

–

PETER MATURI

This narrow shop is rammed with every kind of kitchen implement you could ever need, from "artisan" food blenders and chef's knives to Le Creuset pots and pans.

56 King St, M2 4LY (CC)
petermaturi.com

–

MANCHESTER CRAFT [1] & DESIGN CENTRE

Housed inside a former Victorian market hall, studios cluster around a central, light-filled atrium; some of the North's best designer-makers offer a tempting array of craft, jewellery and accessories.

17 Oak St, M4 5JD (NQ)
craftanddesign.com

–

BEERMOTH

A relative newcomer to the Northern Quarter, Beermoth specialises in contemporary craft beers, many of which are made in Manchester (such as ales from the Marble Arch brewery).

70 Tib St, M4 1LG (NQ)
beermoth.co.uk

–

PICCADILLY RECORDS [2]

This Manchester institution not only stocks one of the best selections of vinyl in the city; its knowledgeable staff and vast online store are worth writing home about, too.

53 Oldham St, M1 1JR (NQ)
piccadillyrecords.com

–

FRED ALDOUS

This design and craft shop, stationers and haberdashers has been trading since 1886; it stocks over 20,000 craft items, from pens and Moleskine notebooks to oil paints and watercolours.

37 Lever St, M1 1LW (NQ)
fredaldous.co.uk

–

MANCHESTER
INTERNATIONAL
FESTIVAL

World Premières & Special Events
Made for Manchester
Shared with the World

mif.co.uk

f mcrintfestival
🐦 @MIFestival

The Perfect Shopping Trip...

Located off central Deansgate, Spinningfields is Manchester's trendy hangout and shopping getaway.

Not only is Spinningfields renowned for its bustling restaurants and annual events programme; The Avenue is also fast becoming the ultimate destination for a retail getaway.

The place where shoppers and party goers come to unwind in some of the city's best restaurants and bars, including the award winning Australasia, an iconic building situated below Emporio Armani, Manchester's quirky pub, The Oast House and Spinningfields' new kid on the block, Neighbourhood.

With an impressive array of shops including Mulberry, Flannels, Oliver Sweeney and more, you'll be sure to find key wardrobe pieces, occasion wear and accessories to satisfy your spree.

Follow us online for the latest shopping and event information @*spinningfields*

SPINNINGFIELDSonline.com   *The Avenue/*

harveynichols.com

HARVEY NICHOLS
THE NEW BREED
WITH J BRAND, EQUIPMENT, SOPHIE HULME

EXCHANGE SQUARE · MANCHESTER

Eat

Brunch and lunch, afternoon tea, casual,
fine dining or just on the hoof.

Hungry? Sit down, you've come to the right place. Manchester is a famously hospitable city - and that hospitality may be best experienced in its kitchens. The restaurant scene here covers all the bases plus some you didn't know existed, from lick-the-plate-they're-so-good burgers to the hautest of the haute cuisine. Whether you're after a sausage barm made with local pork, an Icelandic coffee house, an artisan pizza topped with portobello mushrooms or a six-course paired tasting menu fit to make a foodie swoon, we can help you out. Where else can you jump-start your day with the greasy spoon breakfast that has fuelled untold numbers of indie anthems, linger over lunch at a canal-side gastropub in Castlefield, get a cake and caffeine fix in the arty cafés of the Northern Quarter and then dine in style high above the cityscape? If you don't find a place to eat your fill here, you just haven't looked hard enough.

Image Left: Home Sweet Home, Edge Street

It may be the most important meal of the day but it's easy
enough to miss. Make up for a lost meal by kicking off your city
visit in an eatery specialising in breakfast, brunch or even, for
the lie-in lovers among you, a Sunday lunch. From an American
diner to a full English at an Italian, and from a riverside pub to
lazy mornings at an art-house cinema, these are a few of our
favourite ways to wake up.

HOME SWEET HOME

A homely eatery that majors in American diner-style breakfasts, from waffles and maple porridge to bagels and milkshakes.
49-51 Edge St, M4 1HE (NQ)
cheeseburgertoastie.co.uk

-

NEIGHBOURHOOD

If you're after a New York eatery in the centre of Manchester, look no further. The exuberant, glitzy décor forms the backdrop to brunches crafted from sourdough soldiers and buttermilk pancake stacks.
The Avenue, M3 3HU (SF)
neighbourhoodrestaurant.co.uk

-

MR THOMAS' CHOP HOUSE [3]

This is a splendidly-preserved Victorian pub, its glazed tile-work a joy to behold. In keeping with its original decor, hearty, traditional Sunday roasts are served to appreciative diners.
52 Cross St, M2 7AR (CC)
tomschophouse.com

-

KOFFEE POT

Park yourself in one of the red 'pleather' booths belonging to this fashionably greasy spoon; the eclectic mix of breakfast options includes Mexican-themed tortillas and US-style steak and eggs.
21 Hilton St, M1 1JJ (NQ)
thekoffeepot.co.uk

-

KATSOURIS [2]

A 7am start (8am & 9am weekends), unpretentious vibe and an all-day breakfast menu makes this the perfect place to wake up – whatever time that happens to be.
113 Deansgate, M3 2BQ (DG)
katsourisdeli.co.uk

-

SAN CARLO CICCHETTI

You know how some places exude glamour? This is one of them. Feast on gourmet eats (and arguably the best full English in town) at this chic Italian eatery.
House of Fraser, King St West, M3 2QG (CC)
sancarlocicchetti.co.uk

-

CORNERHOUSE [1]

The city's beloved art-house cinema also offers up a fine Sunday brunch, from mushrooms on toast to veggie breakfasts; bag a window seat and indulge in people-watching as you eat.
70 Oxford St, M1 5NH (OR)
cornerhouse.org

-

THE MARK ADDY

This riverside pub is a master of the sort of meaty, big British classics that could easily soak up most of Sunday.
Stanley St, M3 5EJ (SA)
markaddy.co.uk

While we would never suggest that you organise your whole life around eating, an afternoon in Manchester can be most pleasantly broken up by tea, coffee and cake – served on stands, in towering piles and with a short, sharp caffeine shock that powers you through the rest of the day. Or you might prefer a deli-style snack and finger sandwiches served against the backdrop of crisp, white linen. Whatever you choose, our recommendations allow you to have your cake and eat it.

– Afternoon Tea & Coffee –

TAKK

Named for the Icelandic word for "thanks", this super-stylish coffee house serves up Icelandic art and board games alongside sandwiches, coffee and made-in-Whalley-Range cakes.

6 Tariff St, M1 2FF (NQ)

–

AUBAINE

French-inspired decadence can be found in the form of this second-floor restaurant with views over Exchange Square; its patisserie serves up the finest millefeuille (vanilla slices) in Manchester.

1 Exchange Sq, M3 1BD (CC)
aubaine.co.uk

–

THE MIDLAND

A Manchester institution, this 100-year-old hotel serves afternoon tea in the Moorish-influenced Octagon Lounge, a high-vaulted hideaway that is both grand and glam.

Peter St, M60 2DS (CC)
qhotels.co.uk

–

RICHMOND TEA ROOMS

Step through the looking glass into an Alice in Wonderland-themed tea room – you'll be hard pushed to find anywhere as beautifully quirky as this.

Richmond St, M1 3HZ (GV)
richmondtearooms.com

TEACUP ON THOMAS STREET [2]

Towering piles of homemade cakes, a 23-strong tea list and table-top timers to ensure your loose-leaf brews are perfectly timed all make Teacup terribly popular with afternoon tea-ers.

55 Thomas St, M4 1NA (NQ)
teacupandcakes.com

–

THE SCULPTURE HALL CAFÉ

Shelter in the majestic neo-Gothic Town Hall; take tea (and cake) among the marble statuary of Manchester's great and the good in its atmospheric café.

Town Hall, Albert Sq, M60 2LA (CC)
manchester.gov.uk/townhall

–

NORTH TEA POWER [3]

A tea shop that boasts the city's "first espresso machine tea" comes with a serious selection of teas, addictive cakes, free WiFi and industrial-chic interiors.

36 Tib St, M4 1LA (NQ)
northteapower.co.uk

–

RADISSON BLU EDWARDIAN [1]

Traditional afternoon tea served in a sumptuous setting; the Gentleman's Tea menu, with robust offerings such as mini Yorkshire puds and "rustic" sandwiches, is an interesting touch.

Free Trade Hall, M2 5GP (CC)
radissonblu-edwardian.com

Manchester is famous for being a city that doesn't like to dress up – for anyone. And so it follows that the city's casual dining scene is peppered with the sorts of places in which you can enjoy an evening meal with good surrounds, fine food and fine wines all guaranteed. Booking is sometimes required, sometimes not: if you like to roll with the punches, take your chances and stroll up to some of our favourite places.

SECOND FLOOR RESTAURANT, BAR & BRASSERIE AT HARVEY NICHOLS [2]

With views over the city and a menu that includes hoisin duck with blood orange salad and sea trout with hummus, lentils and yogurt, this eatery offers excellent dining in refined surrounds.

21 New Cathedral St, M1 1AD (CC)
harveynichols.com

–

RED CHILLI

This is a restaurant with a mission: to enhance your experience of Chinese food by looking after your pocket, stomach and soul. Its two Manchester outlets specialise in Beijing and Sichuan dishes.

403-419 Oxford Rd, M13 9WL (OR)
70-72 Portland St, M1 4GU (CT)
redchillirestaurant.co.uk

–

BAKERIE

As easy and unpretentious as its freshly baked bread and vast wine list, Bakerie satisfies all-comers with its simple, carbs-based menu. See also sister venues Pie & Ale and Apotheca.

43-45 Lever St, M60 7HP (NQ)
bakerie.co.uk

–

DUKES 92 [3]

Surrounded by cobbles and canals, Dukes 92 boasts two bars, a grill and canal-side terrace. Famous for its slab-like cheese and paté platters (choose from 40 types of cheese), Dukes is best enjoyed on a sunny afternoon.

18 Castle St, M3 4LZ (CF)
dukes92.com

–

BYRON BURGERS

This is a burger chain, but not as you know it. Byron's serves self-styled "proper burgers" and fries that are pretty damn fine; the industrial-chic surrounds are as carefully crafted, too.

115 Deansgate, M3 2NW (DG)
byronhamburgers.com

–

THE OAST HOUSE [1]

No, your eyes do not deceive you: this is indeed a 16th-century Kentish hop kiln, relocated to Manchester and with its kitchen outside rather than in. Excellent, barbeque-heavy food and cask ales temper its architectural oddity.

The Avenue Courtyard, M3 3AY (SF)
theoasthouse.uk.com

–

EL RINCON DE RAFA

This long-standing eatery serves up authentic Spanish tapas and proper paella – and, despite its back-street location, is worth tracking down.

Off St Johns St, 244 Deansgate,
M3 4BQ (DG)

–

YUZU

Wash down the made-from-scratch Japanese fare and fresh sashimi on offer with rare Japanese beers and specially-selected sake. An authentic taste of the Far East.

39 Faulkner St, M1 4EE (CT)
yuzumanchester.co.uk

We know what it's like. One minute you have all the time in the world, the next you're in a mad spin and late for everything. Luckily, there are plenty of dining options that mean that eating in a hurry is entirely possible. Whether you can spare ten minutes to slurp a soup or need something to eat on the run, there's no need to limit yourself to that same old supermarket sandwich. Read on for our instant hits.

HO'S BAKERY [2]

Ho's was the first Chinese bakery in Manchester's Chinatown back in 1980 and is still the first choice for many seeking traditional Hong Kong-inspired sweet and savoury patisseries.
46 Faulkner St, M1 4FH (CT)
hosbakery.co.uk

–

SLICE [1]

With dough made on the premises from an own-blend flour, and an oven shipped over from Italy, proper, fresh pizza doesn't get much better. As the name suggests, it's sold by the slice.
1a Stevenson Sq, M1 1DN (NQ)
slicepizza.co

–

SHLURP!

Shlurp has spent the past ten years finessing the art of freshly-made fast food: soups, stews, casseroles, salads and sandwiches - there's everything here for someone on the move.
Brazennose St, M2 5BP (CC)
shlurp.co.uk

–

PANCHO'S BURRITOS

Enrique Martinez served more than 50,000 burritos last year. His secret? Recipes from his family in Mexico City. If you're not a fan of burritos, try the flautas, quesadillas or tortillas.
Manchester Arndale Food Market,
M4 3AH (CC)
panchosburritos.co.uk

–

FRESCO FREDDO'S [3]

The cold stuff served here is not ice cream but Italian gelato – a lower fat, creamier version, sold in a dizzying array of flavours.
83 Oxford St, M1 6EG (OR)
frescofreddo.co.uk

–

KEBABISH

If you've a hankering for grilled Pakistani and Indian food, seared over a charcoal grill, head north out of town to this, the home of "apna style" (our style) dishes. Everything is cooked to order.
170-172 Cheetham Hill Rd,
M8 8LQ (CC)
kebabishoriginal-ch.co.uk

–

SALVI'S MOZZARELLA BAR

Open all hours, this family-run deli imports its cheese from Milan and its mozzarella paninis are a revelation; eat inside or take away.
The Corn Exchange, M4 3TR (CC)

–

BOOTHS

This family-run supermarket works with local suppliers, bringing such delicious morsels as Morecambe Bay potted shrimp, damson jelly and Wensleydale cheese to MediaCityUK.
The Garage, MediaCityUK,
M50 2BS (QU)
booths.co.uk

–

Looking to impress? Step this way. Whether you're after a tasting menu with matched wines, have a thing for local, in-season produce or want to seek out a chef with a Michelin star to their name (and the reputation to match), Manchester's myriad fine dining establishments have something to please the most demanding of gastronomes. From French to Modern British, via fusion, Asian or just plain good, here are our tips for places where the food on your plate is the main attraction.

MICHAEL CAINES AT ABODE

With arguably the finest tasting menu in town, the innovative European dishes plated up here make best use of local and regional produce – graze, taste or try the full shebang.
107 Piccadilly, M1 2BD (PD)
michaelcaines.com

–

THE FRENCH

Simon Rogan's restaurant at The Midland has swiftly become one of the city's best; expect native English food, thoughtfully sourced and inventively cooked.
The Midland Hotel, Peter St,
M60 2DS (CC)
the-french.co.uk

–

AUSTRALASIA [2]

A subterranean gem in upmarket Spinningfields, the blonde wood décor provides the backdrop to a menu based on a fusion of modern Australian, Pacific Rim and South East Asian cuisine.
1 The Avenue, M3 3AP (SF)
australasia.uk.com

–

TNQ

A self-styled provider of "gutsy and thought-provoking" food, this dining room is an ideal place to sample seasonal ingredients; its gourmet nights are also worth a gander.
108 High St, M4 1HQ (NQ)
tnq.co.uk

–

63 DEGREES

An intimate, family-run eatery, this is the real deal when it comes to authentic French cuisine: the father and son team behind it hail from Paris. Simple dishes, made with flair, plus wines to match.
20 Church St, M4 1PN (NQ)
63degrees.co.uk

–

THE RIVER BAR AND RESTAURANT AT THE LOWRY [3]

Overlooking the River Irwell and part of the five star Lowry Hotel, chow down on beautifully-cooked food in this two AA Rosette restaurant.
50 Dearmans Place, M3 5LH (SA)
thelowryhotel.com

–

THE RESTAURANT BAR & GRILL

Classic, simple dishes with, as the name suggests, an emphasis on grilled meat and fish, are much improved by an all-weather first floor terrace - al fresco dining with a view.
14 John Dalton St, M2 6JR (DG)
individualrestaurants.com

–

JAMIE'S ITALIAN [1]

Jamie Oliver's latest eatery is housed in a former bank, once known as the "King of King Street"; try seafood bucatini or honeycomb cannelloni while admiring the marble-clad pillars of this Grade II-listed building.
100 King St, M2 4WU (CC)
jamieoliver.com/italian/manchester

–

EXPERIENCE MANHATTAN
IN THE HEART OF SPINNINGFIELDS.

BREAKFAST, BRUNCH, LUNCH & DINNER.

For more information & to view our menu visit
www.neighbourhoodrestaurant.co.uk

For reservations call **0161 832 6334** or email
reservations@neighbourhoodrestaurant.co.uk

 @neighbourhood4
f neighbourhoodrestaurant.co.uk

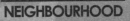

NEIGHBOURHOOD
A NEW YORK INSPIRED
ALL DAY EATERY & BAR

Drink

Pubs, bars, cocktails
and after-hours entertainment.

Fancy a swift one? Encompassing wonders such as
the smallest pub in Europe (Portland Street's wee
Circus Tavern), an emerald testimony to the tiler's
lost art (Peveril of the Peak) and an ingeniously
repurposed underground Victorian public toilet
(The Temple of Convenience), Manchester's historic
pubs are the pride of the city. They also happen to be
the ideal place to encounter the Mancunian in his or
her natural habitat – don't be shy, we're friendly folk.
If you'd prefer something stronger, you'll be happy
to hear that we're undergoing something of a cocktail
renaissance, with a growing army of mixologists
dying to out-do one another with their creations.
They can be enjoyed in settings every bit as
intoxicating as the drinks, from sleek cocktail lounges
and divey rock and roll bars to louche modern-day
gin palaces. Whether your tipple is real ale, craft beer,
cider, wine or spirits, you'll find a warm welcome
in the hostelries of the city.

Image Left: The Alchemist, Hardman Street

1

2   3

There is nothing more quintessentially British than a pint -
apart from perhaps a pint with a packet of pork scratchings.
Manchester knows a thing or two about public houses, from
historic, listed numbers through to the new crop of "craft beer"
outlets that have brought the Victorian boozer bang up-to-date.
In between are pubs that do a good line in food, own-brewed
beer, come with added theatre or are so small you might wonder
how on earth they came to be pubs in the first place.

THE MARBLE ARCH

This Victorian stalwart on the edge of town has just turned 125. Expect local, real ales (brewed by its own Marble microbrewery) alongside a fine seasonal menu. Or try its Northern Quarter sister, 57 Thomas Street.

73 Rochdale Rd, M4 4HY(CC)
marblebeers.com

–

THE BRITONS PROTECTION

A traditional pub beloved of the musicians working at the Bridgewater Hall opposite, this boozer dates back to 1811. It's good for real ale and 300 varieties of whisky.

50 Great Bridgewater St, M1 5LE (DG)
britonsprotectionpub.co.uk

–

PORT STREET BEER HOUSE [1]

This craft beer bar arguably boasts the widest selection of ale in the city, with specialist casks and bottles sourced from across the world – including stellar offerings from Marble Beers.

39-41 Port St, M1 2EQ (NQ)
portstreetbeerhouse.co.uk

–

PEVERIL OF THE PEAK [3]

This is one of Manchester's most distinctive pubs – an award-winning Victorian boozer bedecked with yellow tiles – and is as beautiful on the outside as it is in. It's also alleged to be haunted.

127 Great Bridgewater St,
M1 5JQ (CC)

–

THE KING'S ARMS

A real ale pub that does a fine line in comedy and music, the King's Arms is also home to theatre company, Studio Salford. The bar, meanwhile, played a starring role in Channel 4 comedy, Fresh Meat.

11 Bloom St, M3 6AN (SA)
kingsarmssalford.com

–

THE MOLLY HOUSE [2]

This CAMRA favourite reveals a more grown-up side to Canal Street; a vintage-styled pub that serves hand-pulled beer, fine wine and also boasts a 23 variety-strong tea list.

26 Richmond St, M1 3NB (GV)
themollyhouse.com

–

THE TEMPLE

Get friendly with your partners in booze: this former public toilet is an underground drinking den that's most definitely on the "cosy" side. Or try the miniscule Circus Tavern on nearby Portland Street, a listed pub that's one of Europe's smallest.

100 Great Bridgewater St,
M1 5JW (OR)

–

CASK

Cask's bright blue corner shop frontage belies a cracking bar that serves up continental bottles alongside hand-pulled beers. Its proximity to a chip shop, and encouragement to bring your own food, makes for boozy heaven.

29 Liverpool Rd, M3 4NQ (CF)

–

1
2
3

Looking for a more lively drink or three? Manchester's bar and cocktail scene won't leave you wanting. From bespoke cocktails at the indie bars that occupy the Northern Quarter through to the shimmering rows of rare spirits that line the shelves at high class joints, via odd ingredients (dry ice, anyone?) and award-winning mixologists, here are our recommendations for making a night of it.

– Bars & Cocktails –

COMMON [2]

Common does more than offer hand-pulled beverages: food, cocktails and coffee satisfy most needs, while regular exhibitions, DJ sets and events make it the hang-out of choice for local creatives.

39-41 Edge St, M4 1HW (NQ)
aplacecalledcommon.co.uk

–

THE ALCHEMIST

Bored of the same old drinks? Look no further. From cocktails served in smoking teacups and "sharing kettles" to ingredients such as dried rose buds and dry ice, magical mixology is a regular occurrence here.

3 Hardman St, M3 3HF (SF)
thealchemist.uk.com

–

BREWDOG [1]

Belonging to a Scottish craft brewers, this industrial-chic bar majors on preservative-free, long-brewed beer, including a few that top 30% proof (served as shots).

35 Peter St, M2 5BG (DG)
brewdog.com

–

APOTHECA

The antique pharmacy cabinets and plush furnishings signal that Apotheca takes cocktail-making very seriously indeed; pizza is supplied by neighbour (and sister venture), Dough.

17 Thomas St, M4 1FS (NQ)
apothecabar.co.uk

TERRACE NQ

A new entry onto the late-night scene, Terrace NQ looks and feels like it is set to stay: bare brick walls and industrial lighting form the backdrop to music and DJ sets which have this place heaving.

43 Thomas St, M4 1NA (NQ)

–

CLOUD 23 [3]

Cocktails here come with a view, courtesy of the floor-to-ceiling windows of this recently refurbished Hilton "sky bar". Drinks come with an Industrial Revolution flavour – Berry Black Smog, anyone? Book ahead.

Beetham Tower, M3 4LQ (DG)
cloud23bar.com

–

CORRIDOR

A secret drinking den that has some impressive mixology going on behind its unmarked doors, Corridor boasts a 40-strong cocktail list that has, quite rightly, won it all manner of awards.

6 Barlow's Croft, M3 5DY (SA)
corridorbar.co.uk

–

THE WHISKEY JAR

This two-storey former textiles warehouse has been converted into a bar; its whiskey selection is supplemented by a basement that's carving out a name for live music and DJ sets.

14 Tariff St, M1 2FF (NQ)
thewhiskeyjar.com

1

2

3

Extend your evening in Manchester with an after hours joint
that does more than rustle up a drink or two. Fancy some retro
bowling? We can do that. Want to try your hand at the evening
sport du jour, ping pong? We can do that too. Or, if you want
live music, pool, jazz and DJs, well, whatever your nocturnal
hankerings, Manchester can oblige. The choice is almost endless
– here are our picks to take you through to the small hours.

– After Hours –

ALL STAR LANES [2]

Bowling ain't what it used to be: boutique bowling is the way forward. At this Manchester version of a popular London group, expect home-cooked food, cocktails and private bowling rooms.

The Great Northern, 235 Deansgate, M3 4EN (DG)
allstarlanes.co.uk

–

KOSMONAUT [3]

Stateside speakeasy-style comes to Manchester in the form of Kosmonaut. Sit in a red leather barber's chair while you drink or head to the basement for ping pong parties and DJ sets.

10 Tariff St, M1 2FF (NQ)
kosmonaut.co

–

THE COMEDY STORE

A national comedic institution, this is the only branch of the Comedy Store outside of London; good for new talent as well as established performers.

Deansgate Locks, M1 5LH (WS)
thecomedystore.co.uk

–

BIG HANDS

Big Hands is a great place to spot rock and pop types thanks to its proximity to Manchester Academy. Regular live music and DJs make this an essential indie watering hole.

296 Oxford Rd, M13 9NS (OR)

BLACK DOG BALLROOM

Pool tables and gourmet burgers sit cheek by jowl with cocktails and a private ballroom. Let your hair down here until 4am. Or try its bowling brother, Dog Bowl.

Tib St, M4 1PW (NQ)
blackdogballroom.co.uk

–

THE LIARS CLUB

Descend the stairs and discover the most extensive collection of rum in the North West. Cocktails in coconut shells abound, served up against a backdrop of reggae and afrobeat.

19a Back Bridge St, M3 2PB (CC)
theliarsclub.co.uk

–

G-A-Y

G-A-Y brings one of London's most famous clubs to Canal Street. Loud, proud and, according to some, even better than its big city counterpart, check out the roof terrace and party with a view.

10 Canal St, M1 3WB (GV)
g-a-y.co.uk

–

GORILLA [1]

Like its sister venue, the Deaf Institute, Gorilla offers that rare triptych of entertainment: food, booze (in the form of a gin palace) and a 500-capacity music hall.

54-56 Whitworth St, M1 5WW (WS)
thisisgorilla.com

Music

From clubs to classical, via live venues,
basement dives and arenas.

From the Hallé to the Warehouse Project, Manchester
has a musical pedigree that makes it the envy of
other cities. And while, to some extent, this long and
celebrated history acts as a deadweight it struggles
to shake, the city moves on, reinventing itself every
few years. These days, bands such as Elbow, Delphic
and Everything Everything represent Manchester's
guitar-based music, while the spirit of Factory lives
on through a thriving underground club scene
(see Hoya Hoya, Hit & Run, Drunk At Vogue and
Wet Play), as well as the world-renowned Warehouse
Project. To taste Manchester's current live musical
offering, pay a visit to the impressive Deaf Institute,
jazzy Band on the Wall, intimate Castle Hotel, or new
kid on the block Gorilla; if a huge soundsystem is
more your thing, head to the Berlin-style basement
Soup Kitchen, cavernous Roadhouse, backstreet
dive Kraak or industrial-chic Islington Mill. Or for a
civilised night out, catch the Hallé (155 years young)
or the BBC Philharmonic at the Bridgewater Hall,
RNCM or The Lowry. Whatever your musical taste,
Manchester has it covered.

Image Left: Bridgewater Hall, Lower Mosley Street

1

2

3

The beats and rhymes, the strings and wind, the bleeps and bass: Manchester is not short of a venue or three to house live music gigs - whatever their flavour. With the city home to no less than three national orchestras it's no surprise that it also boasts one of Europe's finest classical concert halls in the shape of the Bridgewater Hall while, close by, RNCM trains up the next generation of classical greats. But the city's established music venues also cater for jazz and world music (take a bow, Band on the Wall) and arena-loving, mainstream acts.

ROYAL NORTHERN COLLEGE OF MUSIC (RNCM)

Although this is a working college, the performances here are never anything less than outstanding, both from current students and the international musicians and specialist festivals it attracts.

124 Oxford Rd, M13 9RD (OR)
rncm.ac.uk

–

BAND ON THE WALL [3]

A major refit in 2009 resulted in the best sound system in the city, but it's the diversity of the bookings that catch the eye at this legendary venue: off-mainstream acts and global cult stars dominate.

25 Swan St, M4 5JZ (NQ)
bandonthewall.org

–

NIGHT & DAY [2]

Plugging live music for almost as long as anyone can remember (or: 1991), Night & Day's dingy stage remains a safe bet for spotting tomorrow's stars.

26 Oldham St, M1 1JN (NQ)
nightnday.org

–

THE BRIDGEWATER HALL

This place is all about the numbers: it cost £42m, is home to two orchestras and boasts a 5,500-pipe organ, meaning that its 250 mainly classical gigs per year are top of the musical range.

Lower Mosley St, M2 3WS (DG)
bridgewater-hall.co.uk

–

MANCHESTER ACADEMY 1/2/3 & CLUB ACADEMY

Once a force for new music, these venues now tend to focus on the offerings from major labels, though the size of the smaller academies still make for an intimate gig.

Oxford Rd, M13 9PR (OR)
manchesteracademy.net

–

MANCHESTER ARENA

Manchester Arena is vast and its 21,000-capacity size accommodates the biggest stars in pop, TV, comedy and sports.

Hunts Bank, M3 1AR (CC)
men-arena.com

–

MATT & PHRED'S [1]

Manchester's much-loved and only live jazz club also provides legendarily good pizza and cocktails. The cosy interior is the perfect setting for music from local and international musicians.

64 Tib St, M4 1LW (NQ)
mattandphreds.com

–

O2 APOLLO

This Grade II-listed former theatre covers the full entertainments remit, from hip hop and tribute acts, via comedy, rock and pop. Choose from a balcony seat or the sweatier dancefloor below.

Stockport Rd, Ardwick Green, M12 6AP (PD)
o2apollomanchester.co.uk

–

1

2

3

In Manchester you don't have to go far to find a musical experience that ventures deeper than some of the more established venues will allow. If you want underground and electronic you can go from vast warehouse to basement dive in the less than the time it takes to reach 120 beats per minute, while reinvented historic pubs such as the Castle Hotel put on intimate live gigs and bar-room DJ mixes pretty much every night of the week. King of the underground is, inevitably, The Warehouse Project, but venues such as Islington Mill and the Soup Kitchen manage to replicate the warehouse vibe on a pleasingly intimate scale.

– Underground –

THE DEAF INSTITUTE

A dome-shaped music hall provides an enchanting, intimate backdrop to independent live music and scores of club nights. One of the city's best such venues. Its sister venue, Gorilla, is also worth a punt.

135 Grosvenor St, M1 7HE (OR)
thedeafinstitute.co.uk

-

THE CASTLE HOTEL

A 200 year-plus pub with a long musical pedigree, the Castle re-opened in 2009 after a major refurb that kept its historic interiors intact; it's one of the Northern Quarter's best tips for hand-pulled ale and live music.

66 Oldham St, M4 1LE (NQ)
thecastlehotel.info

-

ISLINGTON MILL [2]

From Chicago house and electronica to gigs played in complete darkness and, of course, the annual new music fest, Sounds from the Other City, the mill is nothing if not eclectic.

James St, M3 5HW (SA)
islingtonmill.com

-

RUBY LOUNGE [3]

If you like it loud, guitar-based and sweaty, the Ruby Lounge is the place to head for. Live gigs and decent club nights fill up most nights of the week.

28-34 High St, M4 1QB (NQ)
therubylounge.com

-

THE WAREHOUSE PROJECT

Located near Manchester United's ground, this is an out-of-city club experience on an industrial scale. The fact that its main season only runs for three months a year ups the ante – and guarantees sell-out all-nighters. Also try its annual Parklife Weekender.

Trafford Wharf Rd, M17 1AB (QU)
thewarehouseproject.com

-

SOUP KITCHEN

Communal cafe by day, one of Manchester's best live music and club venues by night, the Soup Kitchen works hard pretty much round the clock.

31 Spear St, M1 1DF (NQ)
soup-kitchen.co.uk

-

ST PHILIP WITH ST STEPHEN [1]

A 19th-century church built by Sir Robert Smirke (see also: the British Museum), St. Philip's is a working church – and also, unusually, a live music venue.

2 Wilton Place, M3 6FR (SA)
salfordchurch.org

-

THE ROADHOUSE

This much-loved basement dive has been reinvigorated of late thanks to an emphasis on new live acts and club nights.

8 Newton St, M1 2AN (NQ)
theroadhouselive.co.uk

-

dog bowl

the new breed

BAR | RESTAURANT
TEN PIN BOWLING

Weekdays 12pm 'til 3am
Weekends from 10am

57 Whitworth St West (Opp. Ritz)
Manchester, M1 5WW

0161 228 2888
dogbowl@blackdogballroom.co.uk

www.blackdogballroom.co.uk

"Strike it lucky
with knockout
cocktails and
tasty chow at
this latest
state-of-the-art
ten-pin deluxe
bowling ally."
METRO

Arts

Contemporary to historic:
art, museums, theatre and film.

Scratch the surface of this city and you'll find culture running beneath, a molten river of creativity that flows through Manchester and turns everything that you see or do here into something memorable. Its galleries are among the best in Britain, underpinned by unrivalled Victorian collections of painting, sculpture and even wallpaper. Its museums contain objects that range from fragments of the New Testament to Egyptian mummies. But if you think this is all about "old" art and culture, think again. The Whitworth and Manchester galleries stage exhibitions by some of the world's brightest contemporary art stars, while emerging art is showcased at Cornerhouse and Castlefield Gallery. Central Library is about to unveil a 21st-century face, The Royal Exchange and The Lowry stage newly-penned plays, and, all around, are festivals and performances - including the incredible biennial Manchester International Festival - that you won't see anywhere else. These are tomorrow's masterpieces, created and staged in Manchester today.

Image Left: Chinese Arts Centre, Thomas Street

Manchester has always been a city on the make, and we mean that in the best possible way. From Industrial Revolution magnates to today's painters, sculptors and writers, the thread that connects them all is the desire to make new work in or for the city. Want to see the latest from a Turner Prize-winning artist? You won't have far to go. Interested in new writing and poetry, or want to see how historic artworks sit alongside more recent creations? Step right this way.

MANCHESTER ART GALLERY [3]

Refurbished in 2002, this is one of the city's favourite art spaces - its Victorian collections, contemporary exhibitions, activities for kids and excellent café proving a draw for all-comers.
Mosley St, M2 3JL (CC)
manchestergalleries.org

–

CORNERHOUSE

The much-loved centre of independent art and cinema is about to get a new HOME nearby. For now, check out exhibitions by the current crop of international artists.
70 Oxford St, M1 5NH (OR)
cornerhouse.org

–

THE WHITWORTH ART GALLERY [1]

Before the Whitworth closes for a £15m development that will see a brand new wing extend into the park, enjoy its trademark mix of historic artworks alongside edgy, contemporary pieces.
Oxford Rd, M15 6ER (OR)
manchester.ac.uk/whitworth

–

THE LOWRY

This Salford arts centre has it all: theatre, music, comedy, galleries… head here for exhibitions that blur the line between art and performance, or shows featuring the centre's namesake artist, L.S. Lowry.
Pier 8, M50 3AZ (QU)
thelowry.com

–

CASTLEFIELD GALLERY [2]

After a narrow escape from closure, this excellent gallery has emerged reborn: expect intelligent exhibitions from the region's leading contemporary artists.
2 Hewitt St, M15 4GB (WS)
castlefieldgallery.co.uk

–

ISLINGTON MILL

Edgy, eclectic and art-school cool, this former textiles warehouse packs in galleries, studios, music gigs and the annual Sounds from the Other City festival. Check ahead for opening times.
James St, M3 5HW (SA)
islingtonmill.com

–

INTERNATIONAL ANTHONY BURGESS FOUNDATION

This library and archive centre is dedicated to the work of its namesake author. It also hosts regular events by both new and established writers and poets.
3 Cambridge St, M1 5BY (OR)
anthonyburgess.org

–

CHINESE ARTS CENTRE

Bolstered by a tiny tea shop, the gallery here hosts regular residencies and exhibitions of work by international artists of Chinese heritage.
Thomas St, M4 1EU (NQ)
chinese-arts-centre.org

1

2

3

If your idea of culture leans more towards the historic, may
we point you to Manchester's myriad museums, libraries and
buildings of note? From the world's oldest public library to a
place that has documented Britain's 200-year march towards
democracy, and from a Victorian museum whose Gothic interior
would make Harry Potter feel at home to a venue designed
by one of the world's best-known architects - take your pick.

CHETHAM'S LIBRARY & SCHOOL OF MUSIC

Founded in 1653, this is the oldest public library in the English-speaking world; it's all dark wood interiors, gated bays and ancient tomes chained to shelves. It's also the place where Karl Marx wrote the Communist Manifesto.

Long Millgate, M3 1SB (CC)
chethams.org.uk

–

MANCHESTER MUSEUM [1]

A Victorian natural history museum set up along Darwinian lines, this museum has been re-worked as a 21st century affair, its six million objects displayed in eclectic, clever ways. And there's a full-size T-Rex skeleton, too.

Oxford Rd, M13 9PL (OR)
manchester.ac.uk/museum

–

NATIONAL FOOTBALL MUSEUM [3]

After a significant refurb in 2012, the former Urbis reopened with a splash - in its first year around half a million people visited the new home of British football.

Urbis, M4 3BG (CC)
nationalfootballmuseum.com

–

PEOPLE'S HISTORY MUSEUM

One of three national museums in the city and the only one in the country that tells the 200-year story of the British march to democracy – which it does, in spades.

Left Bank, M3 3ER (SF)
phm.org.uk

–

THE JOHN RYLANDS LIBRARY

Considered by some to be one of the finest libraries in the world, this is a neo-Gothic wonder whose wood-panelled reading room is a highlight of literary Manchester.

150 Deansgate, M3 3EH (DG)
manchester.ac.uk/library

–

CENTRAL LIBRARY

This neo-Classical, circular library echoes the civic grandeur of the neighbouring Town Hall and Manchester Art Gallery - it emerges from a £48m renovation in 2014.

St Peter's Sq, M2 5PD (CC)
manchester.gov.uk

–

MOSI, MUSEUM OF SCIENCE & INDUSTRY [2]

Have kids? Like trains, planes and automobiles? Head here for your science and steam fix; the children's interactive gallery benefitted from a major refit in 2011 and is an inspirational playground.

Liverpool Rd, M3 4FP (CF)
mosi.org.uk

–

IWM NORTH

This Daniel Libeskind-designed museum shimmers by the side of the Manchester Ship Canal; award-winning for architecture, exhibitions and its collection, it also supplies a dizzying vista via its viewing tower.

Trafford Wharf Rd, M17 1TZ (QU)
iwm.org.uk

–

Are you sitting comfortably? Then let's begin with some highlights of Manchester's spectacular theatre and film scene. The city is rich in performance – if you love West End musicals or classic theatre you need not look far to find something to delight. If, however, you live for world premieres and new work by emerging playwrights, well, you won't have to search too hard for that either. And, from art-house to blockbuster, cinema in the city is just as diverse.

– Theatre & Film –

THE ROYAL EXCHANGE [2]

It's almost worth a visit just to see the "spaceship" structure of this remarkable theatre space. Revel in its record for revitalizing classics starring big names and, increasingly, spotlighting new talent.
St Ann's Sq, M2 7DH (CC)
royalexchange.co.uk

–

PALACE THEATRE [1]

Plush, mainstream, popular and well-run, the Palace is usually the first call when blockbuster musicals such as The Lion King venture outside London.
97 Oxford St, M1 6FT (CC)
manchesterpalace.org.uk

–

CONTACT THEATRE

Youth-orientated and buzzing with energy at most hours of the day, this is a place to catch cutting-edge talent, sometimes still raw but always exciting.
Oxford Rd, M15 6JA (OR)
contact-theatre.org

–

THE LOWRY

This forward-looking venue has lovingly championed dance and new writing but also brings shows from the likes of The Donmar and the RSC to town, along with the blockbusters.
Pier 8, M50 3AZ (SA)
thelowry.com

–

THE OPERA HOUSE

In its 100-year history, stars from Laurence Olivier to Vivien Leigh and Kenneth Branagh have trodden the boards of this classic theatre and it still attracts top entertainment names.
3 Quay St, M3 3HP (SF)
manchesteroperahouse.org.uk

CORNERHOUSE [3]

Known for its art-house films as much as for its art, there are great expectations for Cornerhouse's alliance with the Library Theatre Company in their shared new home, HOME – opening in 2015.
70 Oxford St, M1 5NH (OR)
cornerhouse.org

–

AMC GREAT NORTHERN

Competitively-priced, high-spec, 16-screen cinema, complete with late-night shows in a leisure, retail and entertainment complex, housed in a historic Grade II-listed Victorian warehouse.
235 Deansgate, M3 4EN (DG)
amccinemas.co.uk

–

ODEON PRINTWORKS

The Printworks itself is a busy collection of bars and clubs, and within it lies this vibrant multi-screen cinema which embraces new technology such as IMAX and 3D.
27 Withy Grove, M4 2BS (CC)
odeon.co.uk

–

Stay

Business, budget and groups,
top end hotels and boutique stays.

There is no shortage of places to stay in Manchester – well, not unless you turn up on one of those rare evenings where football and pop music collide, and the hotels are chock-full of fans of both the sporting and musical variety. More likely, you'll pitch up here and find a diverse array of hotels that supply more than just a roof over your head. At the top end of the market are the newly-built or recently scrubbed-up hostelries that come with staggering views (such as the 47-storey Hilton Hotel), feature some of the city's best restaurants (Simon Rogan's The French at The Midland), boast five stars (The Lowry Hotel) or have a history so fascinating you could dedicate a book to them. Of the latter, The Midland and the former Free Trade Hall, now the Radisson Blu Edwardian, are our favourites. But if your wallet won't stretch to multi-star delights there are plenty of cheaper options, with families and groups willingly catered for via a growing number of apart-hotels and budget places to stay which, like so much of Manchester, come with unexpected extras.

Image Left: Great John Street Hotel, Great John Street

– Business, Budget & Groups –

MACDONALD MANCHESTER HOTEL & SPA

A 4-star hotel within easy walking distance of Piccadilly Station, it boasts an AA rosette-holding restaurant and has been voted one of Europe's best for business travellers.

London Road, M1 2PG (PD)
macdonaldhotels.co.uk

–

THE OXNOBLE

The ten, en-suite rooms above this award-winning gastropub offer excellent value for money; the "modern Victorian" interiors of the pub extend to its pleasing bedrooms.

71 Liverpool Rd, M3 4NQ (CF)
theox.co.uk

–

ROOMZZZ APARTHOTEL

The luxury apartments here boast soaring interior spaces and kitchens equipped with Smeg appliances. There's also room service and complimentary "grab and go" breakfast.

36 Princess St, M1 4JY (CT)
roomzzz.co.uk

–

DOUBLETREE BY HILTON HOTEL

A hair's breadth from Piccadilly Station (a pedestrian bridge links station to hotel), this has everything you'd expect from a city centre hotel: decent restaurant, iMacs in every room, flexible check-in and 24-hour room service.

1 Auburn St, M1 3DG (PD)
doubletree3.hilton.com

–

PLACE APARTMENT HOTEL

The spacious four-star accommodation (numbering 107 loft apartments) recently benefitted from a £1.5m refit while its status as a converted Grade II-listed warehouse means plenty of original features.

Ducie St, M1 2TP (PD)
theplacehotel.com

–

LIGHT APARTHOTEL

With apartments, an on-site gym and two penthouse suites complete with their own rooftop jacuzzis, there is much to like here. Kitchens come with Bosch appliances; bedrooms boast Egyptian cotton sheets.

20 Church St, M4 1PN (NQ)
thelight.co.uk

–

SACO MANCHESTER

These stylish studio, one and two bedroom apartments boast floor to ceiling windows, on site parking and 24-hour reception, and are minutes from Piccadilly Station.

5 Piccadilly Place, M1 2PF (PD)
sacoapartments.com

–

STAYCITY

Groups of between three and eight are catered for in these 84 serviced apartments, which come with WiFi, linen, towels, kitchens and more.

40 Laystall Street, M1 2JZ (PD)
staycity.com

–

– Top End & Boutique –

THE LOWRY

The 5-star Lowry, with its sublime River Restaurant and celebrity-friendly décor, is a stone's throw from both city centre Manchester and Salford's indie arts scene.

50 Dearmans Place, M3 5LH (SA)
thelowryhotel.com

–

MIDLAND HOTEL

The terracotta and polished exterior of this historic hotel hints at the £1m it cost to build back in 1903; today it remains one of the top-end hotels in the city with excellent dining to boot.

Peter St, M60 2DS (CC)
qhotels.co.uk

–

RADISSON BLU EDWARDIAN

The former Free Trade Hall has a fascinating musical and political past, glimpses of which can be seen in the many retained original features. Like The Midland, it boasts an excellent restaurant .

Peter St, M2 5GP (CC)
radissonblu-edwardian.com

–

GREAT JOHN STREET HOTEL

The city's only top-end boutique hotel; just 30 rooms with features such as walk-in rain showers, twin baths, period furniture and a rooftop hot tub and garden.

Great John St, M3 4FD (CF)
eclectic-hotel-collection.com

–

HILTON

Taking up 23 floors of Manchester's tallest building, Beetham Tower, the Hilton's main draw is the view from its floor to ceiling windows, though its pool, spa and two restaurants are equally impressive.

303 Deansgate, M3 4LQ (DG)
hilton.co.uk

–

ABODE

Set inside a restored, Grade II-listed warehouse, ABode is particularly noteworthy for the loft-style suites on the top floor and, far below, Michael Caines' excellent eatery in the basement.

107 Piccadilly, M1 2DB (PD)
abodehotels.co.uk

–

MALMAISON

The emphasis at this former textile mill turned hotel is firmly on fashionable decadence: boutique-styled suites are plush and mood-lit, with free-standing baths and even a four poster bed on offer.

1-3 Piccadilly, M1 1LZ (PD)
malmaison-manchester.com

–

VELVET

A 19-room boutique hotel in the heart of the Gay Village, the rooms here are individually designed and come with extras such as tuck boxes and double-head rain showers.

2 Canal St M1 3HE (GV)
velvetmanchester.com

–

The leading 5 star hotel in the north west

THE LOWRY HOTEL
MANCHESTER

The Lowry Hotel offers 165 bedrooms, six suites and the Charles Forte Presidential Suite. The hotel is contemporary whilst being luxurious and comfortable.

The River Restaurant offers a classic menu whilst the River Bar and Library offer a modern, light menu throughout the day.

The luxurious **Lowry Spa**, offers a range of treatments from Carita and Elemis, a gym, sauna and relaxation lounges.

Room rates from £169.00 per room
Special menus from £19.50 per person for 3 courses

The Lowry Hotel | 50 Dearmans Place, Chapel Wharf, Salford, Manchester, M3 5LH
Telephone +44 (0) 161 827 4000 Fax +44 (0) 161 827 4001
enquiries.lowry@roccofortehotels.com www.roccofortehotels.com

ROCCO FORTE HOTELS

DoubleTree
BY HILTON
MANCHESTER ~ PICCADILLY

We put back some of what travel takes out

At DoubleTree by Hilton we put the human touch back into your travel experience. It all starts with the warm welcome of a chocolate chip cookie at check-in...

- 285 bedrooms, including 7 suites with contemporary furnishing, iMac's and Crabtree and Evelyn Bathroom products.
- City Café Restaurant offers modern Cuisine in a stylish yet comfortable backdrop.
- Situated right at the heart of the gateway to Manchester, shopping areas such as the Arndale, King Street and Deansgate are just a short walk away.
- Manchester Piccadilly Station is located next to the hotel, providing quick access to the rest of the country and Manchester Airport.

HILTON
WORLDWIDE

1 Auburn Street, Manchester
M1 3DG
0161 242 1000
doubletree.hilton.com/manchester

Stay central
stay in style...

Stay central: Located right in the heart of the City, just five minutes walk from Manchester Piccadilly station.

Stay in style: Stunning Victorian hotel, from the modern lobby to indoor plunge pool.

The meeting venue: Stay connected with free Wi-Fi in nine meeting rooms and across the hotel.

Go explore: Close to the Arndale Centre, Europe's largest city centre shopping mall, The Lowry Museum and Old Trafford.

**Enjoy 10% off with this code: TTT92
Book your stay today.**

Travel well, visit **thistle.com**

thistle

Lobby

Deluxe Bedroom

The Portland Street Bar

Useful info

MANCHESTER VISITOR INFORMATION CENTRE

For full travel, transport and visitor information, as well as Manchester merchandise and one-to-one advice, head here. Open 9.30am-5.30pm Mon-Sat, 10.30am-4.30pm Sun.

Piccadilly Plaza, Portland Street, M1 4AJ (CC)
visitmanchester.com

–

VISIT MANCHESTER

The official destination website for Greater Manchester, this site contains all the information you'd ever need on shopping, events, sport, travel, places to stay, tourist information and more.

visitmanchester.com

–

CREATIVE TOURIST

The creative tourist's guide to Manchester and beyond, this independent, online magazine offers an insider's guide to the best art, culture, food, drink, festivals and more in the rainy city.

creativetourist.com

–

BOOTS

From food to cosmetics via prescription glasses and electrical items, this enormous store has it all – plus an NHS walk-in centre and pharmacy. Open seven days a week.

32 Market Street, M1 1PL (CC)
boots.com

–

SALFORD TOURIST INFORMATION CENTRE

Tucked into The Lowry arts centre, this TIC is open 10am-5.15pm Tue-Fri; 10am-4pm Sat; 11am-5pm Sun (closed Mon).

The Lowry, Pier 8, The Quays, M50 3AZ (QU)
visitsalford.info

–

RYMAN

Need a mobile top-up? Envelopes, stamps, spare cables? A shop for the things that are so useful – and yet so easily left at home. Its university branch is handily close to Manchester Museum.

Manchester Arndale, M4 2HU (CC)
ryman.co.uk

–

MCDONALDS

It may not be top of the gastronome's must-eat list, but the Oxford Street branch is open 24 hours, seven days a week – which has to beat a kebab, surely?

36-38 Oxford Street, M1 5EJ (CC)
mcdonalds.co.uk

–

CITY HOSTS

This team of hosts are on hand in the city centre to help visitors with advice and information – look out for their distinctive black and red uniforms.

Market, King & New Cathedral St and Exchange & St Ann's Sq.

–

Listings Index

Travel

Visitor information.

TRAIN

Piccadilly Station is the city's main rail station. Other stations in the city centre are Victoria, Deansgate and Oxford Road. Main rail operators into and out of Manchester are Virgin Trains (hourly to London; just over two hours), First Transpennine Express, CrossCountry Trains and Northern Rail. For all train travel enquiries, visit nationalrail.co.uk or call 08457 484950.

AIR

Manchester Airport (0871 271 0711, manchesterairport.co.uk) is the busiest UK airport outside London; trains run to and from the airport to Piccadilly Station every 10 minutes (journey approx. 20 minutes).

CAR

For information about parking, visit Manchester City Council's dedicated parking page at manchester.gov.uk/parking or try ncp.co.uk. For taxis, try Manchester Cars (0161 228 3355, ilovemanchestercars.co.uk), Streetcars Private Hire (0161 228 7878, streetcarsmanchester.co.uk) or Union Private Hire (0161 833 4141, unioncarsmanchester.co.uk).

TRAM

Metrolink (0161 205 2000, metrolink.co.uk) is the light rail network that connects Greater Manchester. Services run 7 days a week; check tfgm.com for details. Buy tickets on the platform.

BUS

The Metroshuttle (0161 244 1000, tfgm.com) is a free bus that runs from all city rail stations and connects to shopping districts and businesses in the city centre. There are three circular routes, running every 10 minutes, 7am-7pm Mon-Fri; 8am-7pm Sat (not Sun or BH). National Express coaches (08717 818178, nationalexpress.com) can be found just five minutes' walk from Piccadilly Gardens. Other major bus companies in Manchester include Stagecoach and First Group. Bus timetables and public transport information can be found at **Transport for Greater Manchester** *(tfgm.com).* **System One Travelcard** *information (unlimited travel across bus, train and tram) can be found at systemonetravelcards.co.uk.*

CYCLING

For all information on bicycle lanes, hire, hubs, storage and repair, visit Transport for Greater Manchester's online cycling centre at cycling.tfgm.com

Image Left: Manchester

AUSTRALASIA

MANCHESTER

www.australasia.uk.com

1 The Avenue, Spinningfields, Manchester, M3 3AP
Tel: 0161 831 0288

MANCHESTER
HOUSE

RE
DEFINE
FINE
DINE